# FERRY FINDINGS

## An Anthology of Pacific Northwest Magic

Stories by Susan McDonough-Wachtman

Photos by Glenn Wachtman

Ferry Findings
First edition, published 2016

By Susan McDonough-Wachtman
Photos by Glenn Wachtman

Copyright © 2016, Susan McDonough-Wachtman

ISBN-13: 978-1-942661-30-6

All rights reserved. No part of this book may be reproduced or transmitted in any form or by any means, electronic or mechanical, including photocopying, recording or by any information storage and retrieval system, without written permission from the author, except for the inclusion of brief quotations in a review.

Published by Kitsap Publishing
P.O. Box 572
Poulsbo, WA 98370
www.KitsapPublishing.com

Printed in the United States of America

TD 20160711

50-10 9 8 7 6 5 4 3 2 1

# DEDICATION

*to*

*Tony, Ethan, and Bethany*

*And James, of course*

# CONTENTS

| | |
|---|---:|
| Introduction | 1 |
| Crabby Converse | 2 |
| Ferry Findings | 17 |
| Carson the Heron | 22 |
| Seal Story | 28 |
| Huckleberry Horizon | 33 |
| New Heading | 39 |
| It's Magic | 55 |
| About the Photographer | 65 |
| About the Author | 67 |

# ACKNOWLEDGMENTS

"Crabby Converse" was originally published on Fabula Argentea

http://www.fabulaargentea.com/

"Ferry Findings" was originally published by Literary Mama

http://www.literarymama.com/

"New Heading" was originally published in Shadow

# INTRODUCTION

The Pacific Northwest has been our home all our lives. Glenn's family has deep roots at Priest Lake in Idaho, and he grew up on the waterfront near Southworth, Washington, ten minutes from the ferry dock. Susan's family spent years vacationing on the Washington and Oregon coast and at Lake Cushman in the Olympic Forest of Washington.

You have to appreciate the cool color palette when you live here. Blues, greens and grays predominate; the warmer colors are rare But there is something about the misty water on a chill morning and the cry of a seagull which says: "Be aware. Life is passing -- and it will last forever."

It's a contradictory message that we find comforting.

The stories and the pictures in this anthology are our attempt to express our feeling of the immediacy of joy, the frailty of life, and the longevity of this world.

Susan and Glenn Wachtman

February, 2016

# CRABBY CONVERSE

Beverly decided to walk down to the beach. She knew she wasn't supposed to. She had been given strict orders by her daughter never to attempt the outside stairs without help, let alone to cross the lawn, cross the street or go onto the beach. But.

It was such a beautiful day.

Only rarely in the spring did the Pacific Northwest get a day like this. "It would be a sin to waste this day sitting inside," she said to the picture of her husband, Herb.

He was chuckling. "Oh, it would, would it?" he seemed to say.

"Yes, it would," she replied firmly.

Beverly prepared for her outing. Old polyester slacks. If they got dirty, she wouldn't care. T-shirt, because it was at least 75 degrees. Sweatshirt, because the breeze might be chilly. Scarf tied firmly over her bristly white hair. Sunglasses. Bottle of water. She stopped at the door, knowing she was missing something. Shoes. She sat down on the chair by the door and took off her slippers. She contemplated the two pairs of canvas shoes she kept there. The nicer-looking ones fit better but had to be tied on. Her feet were *such* a long way down. She took the easier course and chose the slip-ons. They were ratty-looking and she wouldn't mind getting them wet.

As she edged her way down the outside stairs, holding on tightly to the iron railing, she reflected that the shoes might have been a mistake. Her feet - praise God - were not a bit swollen or sore today. However, she had worn light socks and the slip-ons were loose. The thought of going back up five stairs and sitting down and changing shoes and coming down the five stairs.... no. She continued her careful shuffle and made it safely to the bottom. Ha!

She stood for a minute, catching her breath and looking out at the water. The ferry to Vashon Island was passing, a few seagulls accompanying it. Someone must be feeding them. She could see no white caps at all, not even on the unprotected waters beyond Yukon Harbor. She was glad she had worn the T-shirt. A shadow passed over her and she looked up to see a kingfisher land on the telephone wire. He perched there, contemplating the water.

"Good luck," Beverly called up to him. Now, where was her walking stick? Argh. All the way across the carport. A grandchild must have been playing with it. Probably James, who would wear his brown robe and pretend to be Gandalf. She shuffled carefully across the cement floor and grasped the smooth wood with relief. Now she could attempt the lawn. The neighbors must have been mowing. The air smelled of freshly cut grass and lilacs.

Beverly tilted her head back and scanned the sky. No eagles, no ospreys, no hawks, no herons. Just a couple of seagulls and a crow. She lowered her head and applied herself to the task at hand. She could hear Herb's voice: "Would you *please* stop looking at the sky and watch where you're going?"

"Yes, yes," she muttered as she marched across the lawn. "If you'd put in the path I wanted years ago, this would be easier. All this lawn makes no sense." It was an old argument which she had seen no reason to terminate simply because he was dead. "Look at those geese on the neighbors' lawn. That's all a lawn is good for."

"And you like watching the geese!" her husband would say.

It was true. They could be nasty creatures, but the rarely seen goslings were a delight. And there was something about the self-confidence of the mature geese which appealed to her. Like crows. So cocky and sure of themselves. And the blue herons, which reminded her of English butlers. She always called herons "Jeeves" or "Carson."

She had reached the road. She stopped, panting a little as she looked both ways. It had been so much less busy when the kids had been young. She worried constantly about the grandkids when they were on the beach. When the ferry traffic came through, their formerly quiet street was like a highway. No traffic now, though. She marched across, imagining that she looked like a goose -- rear end waddling. Not that she was fat, but things did tend to sag, no matter how much she tried to exercise.

When she reached the safety of the other side she stopped and looked back. Was she being observed? It was the middle of a work day, so most of the neighbors would be gone. But there were some who might feel it their civic duty to call Beverly's daughter and report this forbidden activity. There were advantages and disadvantages to having lived in the same place for forty years. Her daughter had said, "I've asked the

Stanleys to keep an eye on you. I don't want you to go down to the beach at all, but I know you will, so I'll put in a railing."

Her daughter had done just that last summer. Beverly had looked into her daughter's eyes and bitten back her sharp retort. Behind her daughter's pomposity, Beverly had seen the love and worry.

Beverly edged her way down the boat ramp, hanging onto the railing on the left side, and stepped, at last, onto the pebbly beach. She drew a deep breath of pride and sea air. Salt water, seaweed, fish -- they had been the scent of home all her life. She had never wanted to live anywhere but the Pacific Northwest. She liked to travel, but this was home. Her daughter wanted her to move into a nursing home, and Beverly knew it would be necessary soon. But not quite yet, please God. Not quite yet.

Beverly edged her way alongside the ramp until it was high enough for her to prop her butt against it. She rested there, looking down at the dried seaweed and rough sand, broken shells, rocks, driftwood and bits of broken glass. The sun was glinting on the water so brightly it was hard to look at even through her sunglasses. She could see Mount Baker very faintly in a far-off haze. A couple of sailboats passed in front of Blake Island. Old pilings to her left were all that remained of the business that had been done here -- long before her time -- in lumber and bricks and fishing. One brown gull bobbed past her.

A bit of a walk, Beverly told herself -- and then she had to argue with her husband about it. "I won't go far," she promised him, "just to the pilings."

"Remember that you have to come back again!" he insisted.

"Stop nagging!"

She shuffled carefully over the pebbles, cursing her loose shoes. Below her feet, dried seaweed and sand, broken shells, rocks of all sizes, pieces of brick, driftwood, seaweed of tan, green, brown, red, broken glass in various stages of polish, dead crabs --- ooooh. Beverly flinched back in surprise as a moon snail shell moved and a hermit crab scuttled in front of her. Beverly's floppy shoe went one way and her foot the other. She slammed her stick into the ground on the water side, trying to regain her balance, but the stick hit a barnacle-clad rock instead and stuck, then slipped. With a screech and a howl, Beverly crashed to her side where she lay, gasping, wondering if anything was broken.

Her head was ringing a bit, but she could still see clearly. She was angled toward the water, and her feet were up the beach. The slope was slight, but there was a definite tilt to her body. Her walking stick was half underneath her, as was the pocket which held the water bottle. She could feel them digging into her side. Her sunglasses had come off and lay, one lens cracked, about a foot away -- right next to the crab. Beverly eyed it with disfavor. "This is all your fault."

"I beg your pardon?"

Beverly blinked. Conversations with her husband, she figured, were a not-unreasonable eccentricity for an elderly widow. Talking to a hermit crab, however... "Did you... speak?"

The hermit crab stepped out of his shell, and approached her. Beverly pulled her head back uneasily.

"I feel it necessary to defend myself," said the crab with dignity. "You invaded my territory AND you nearly stepped on me, and you conclude it is MY fault that you fell?"

Beverly closed her eyes. Clearly she had hit her head harder than she had realized. Keeping her eyes closed, she took inventory, making slight movements of all extremities. Everything seemed to be working without any more than the usual arthritic pain. Her head ached, but she wasn't aware of any disorientation. She knew she had fallen on her beach, and she knew she needed to get up before the tide came in. "I need to get up," she said.

"Please do," said the small, precise voice.

Beverly opened her eyes. "I've never had a conversation with a crab before," she said with a sigh. "But I suppose there's a first time for everything."

"Cliché," said the crab disapprovingly.

"Excuse me?" It was bad enough to talk to a crab, but to be criticized for what she said was beyond all!

"A trite or overused idea," continued the crab. "An obvious and overused statement." He had large, oval black eyes on short stalks, and white markings on his legs. He was about two inches wide, and the inside of his shell was pearly with an iridescent glow.

Beverly attempted diplomacy. "Your shell is beautiful."

"MUST you say so? I would rather not speak of it."

"But why not? Don't you like it?"

The crab tapped his front leg against a rock petulantly. "Can you not see that I have outgrown it? I must move into a new one, and I am exTREMEly upset about it!"

"Ahh." Leave it to me, Beverly thought, to start up a conversation with an excitable, depressed, melodramatic hermit crab. "Herb," she muttered, "I think I need some help here."

"Who is Herb?"

"For a creature with no discernible ears, you have excellent hearing."

"YOU have poor discernment."

Beverly abandoned diplomacy. "Herb is my husband, and he is far more pleasant to talk to than you are."

The crab tapped his front leg again. "I surmise that Herb is not here."

"Herb is wherever he wishes to be. Herb is dead."

"Then it is not surprising that your conversations with him are pleasant. They are imaginary."

Beverly had had enough. "You are not nice." She attempted to pull her right arm and the walking stick out from under her. She rolled backward and pulled forward, but very little seemed to happen. She was uneasily aware of the rhythmic swish and slurp of the waves approaching her head.

She could hear the buzz of a motorboat, but she knew there was no way they could see her. She had not worn her neon vest, which she was supposed to wear whenever she went in the yard. She could remember when it had been she who had given the orders: "Wear your jacket! If you ride your bike, you must wear your helmet!" A long time ago.

Beverly swallowed thirstily. Maybe she could get her arm out if she let go of the stick? But then how would she get up without the stick? But how would she get up without her arm? She rolled back, let go of the stick and pulled her arm forward a couple of inches. "Agh," she moaned with the sharp pain of it. So she had damaged something, after all. Hard to say just what -- elbow? shoulder? The pain seemed all over her right side now. The water bottle pressing against her side was doubly torturous –- first because it hurt, and second because she was so thirsty.

"Why should I be?"

She had forgotten the crab. "Why should you be what?"

"Nice!"

"Why not? Life is short!" I must be hallucinating, she thought.

"Cliché."

"Have you ever thought about why clichés become clichés?" snapped Beverly. "It's because they are true!"

"A human-centric way of thinking," grumbled the crab. "The sea has been here for millions of years."

"It's all relative," said Beverly. "I know, I know -- cliché. Do you have anything useful to contribute? If not, why don't you go away?"

"Because," said the crab, "you are lying against the shell I was in-TENDing to make my new home."

"Well, I am sorry about that, but I may be here awhile, and I'm sure you can find another."

"Again, a ridiculously human-centric thing to say." The crab tapped his foot on his current home. "Unbroken shells larger than this one are not easy to come by. And unoccupied ones are nearly impossible. I have spent a lot of time cleaning this one -- as you mentioned, it has developed a spectacular sheen due to my labor." He turned around. "I can't talk about this." He went slowly back to the shell and crawled inside.

Beverly could see now that the shell was not large enough for him. No matter how he tried, he could not get all the way inside.

"I am sorry," she said. "My daughter wants me to move out of my home, so I know how you feel."

"And will you have to fight someone for a new one?" he demanded, his back to her, his voice echoing hollowly.

"No, of course not!"

"As I said. Human-centric. Just because you must leave your home, you think you understand my sorrow and fear, but you will not have to risk losing your leg -- or your life -- in acquiring a new home." He turned around. "Will you?"

Beverly was suitably humbled. "That's true."

"Even worse would be if more than one crab hears about my plight. There could be a free-for-all of crabs fighting for new homes, each one hoping to move up to a better standard of living."

"Oh, dear. If you'll excuse my saying so, that seems very uncivilized for a creature as obviously erudite as you are." *Did you hear that, Herb? I used the word 'erudite.' You taught me that one - seven letters, means showing great learning.*

The crab ventured a few steps out of his shell, obviously pleased. "Well," he said, "I am not an average crab."

"I didn't think so." Beverly became aware that the top of her head was a little damp from spray. "Mr. Crab, if you have any suggestions that will get me upright, it would be beneficial for both of us." Beverly attempted to roll again, and the pain made her vision go black for a moment.

"Can you whistle?"

"Pardon me?" she gasped.

"That idiot dog which belongs to your neighbor is currently polluting your yard. If you whistle, he'll probably come and bark at you -- if he doesn't get hit by a car. Either way, it may draw some attention." A seagull landed suddenly by Beverly's head. "Oh, drat," said the crab, and withdrew into his shell as far as he was able.

"Yah! Yah!" screeched Beverly. She flapped her left arm wildly and the seagull squawked and flew off.

"Thank you," said the crab.

"You're welcome. I'm Beverly." She waved her left hand at him.

"I am Winston."

"I will attempt a whistle, but my mouth may be too dry. And if that obnoxious terrier gets hit by a car, I'll feel dreadfully guilty." She tried to whistle but only a squeak emerged from her parched lips.

"Is that a bottle of water?" Winston pointed with his largest claw.

"Yes, but I can't reach it." Beverly attempted again to reach across herself for the stick or the bottle, but she couldn't quite reach either, and she was reluctant to try another roll.

Winston scuttled forward. After several attempts, he managed to get his largest claw clamped around the neck of the bottle. He dragged it forward an inch, then two. Beverly grasped the top with her left hand. She drew it with difficulty to her mouth and twisted the cap off with her teeth. Water spilled out, but she managed to pour some into her mouth. "Ahhhh," she sighed. "Winston, you're a genius."

"Whistle," prompted Winston.

Beverly pursed her lips and after a couple of squeaks produced a shrill whistle. Almost immediately she could hear the terrier yipping excitedly as it came her way. Beverly closed her eyes, praying not to hear the skid of a car. There was none. Winston scrambled into his shell as the dog dashed over to them, sand flying from his small paws, his frantic yelping music to Beverly's ears. Only a few minutes later she heard Mr. Stanley's irritated monologue: "Shut up, you darn dog, what the heck are you doing over here? Boomer, you mutt, you know the wife'll give you grief if she catches you over here, and she'll give me even more grief if you get smacked by a car, so just stop your caterwauling and -- Beverly!"

Beverly closed her eyes and pretended to be unconscious so as not to have to deal with the worried questions and the scolding. There would be enough of that later. Right now she was just too tired. Soon enough Mr. Stanley had called for help on his cell phone, and he went up to the road to signal the ambulance. The terrier bounced back and forth between him and Beverly, unable to stand the excitement of his importance. To her relief, the dog eventually decided he was needed more beside the road, and he ran up, yipping excitedly at every car and being sworn at by Mr. Stanley.

Beverly opened her eyes. "Thank you so much, Winston," she whispered. "I hope I didn't damage your shell."

The crab emerged cautiously. "You didn't. I can see it."

"Well, why don't you get it then?"

"I was going to, but your plight distracted me." If a crab could look sheepish, he did.

"Well, I'm glad of that, but get it now, for heaven's sake. Before the ambulance guys stomp all over here getting me off this beach!"

"I'm afraid of the dog."

"I'll take care of the dog," said Beverly grimly.

Winston came forward and grasped the shell which was just in front of Beverly's thigh. Winston began backing away, towing his prize. Boomer chose this inopportune moment to check on his find and dashed back to Beverly, yelping. Setting her lips determinedly, Beverly raised her left arm and with perfect timing, managed to scoop up the dog as he attempted to run past her. She grasped him close as Winston slipped into his new home and scurried into the water.

"Goodbye, Beverly! Good luck in your new home!"

"You too! And thank you! Thank you, thank you so much!"

"Beverly," cried Mr. Stanley, and she could hear him crunching across the beach. "You're conscious! There's no need to thank the damn dog, he has no idea what he's done! How are you feeling? And what the heck were you doing down here, anyway?"

"Talking to a hermit crab," she said as she let the dog loose.

"WHAT?"

"Finding inner peace," said Beverly.

She could hear other footsteps, and Mr. Stanley said, "I think she's delirious."

"Probably dehydrated," said a new voice.

"I am not a bit dehydrated," said Beverly. "My water bottle is right here." Herb, she thought, I believe I'll be moving out of our home soon. I hope you won't mind.

"Mind?" said Herb, "Why should I mind? Home is just a place to hang your hat!"

"Cliché," murmured Beverly. "And human-centric, too."

**FAMILY DISCUSSION QUESTIONS**

- *What does it feel like to grow older?*
- *Have you ever missed someone who was gone? Have you talked to them even though they were not with you?*
- *What is a cliché? Why doesn't Winston like them?*
- *What do you think it means to be human-centric?*

http://literarydevices.net/cliche/

# FERRY FINDINGS

The fog was lifting and the sun was beginning to hit the water. The ferry rumbled and grumbled and pulled away from the dock. I leaned against the railing and looked down into the water. But I didn't see any jellyfish.

"Get back from that rail, Carla," said my mother. "Do you want to fall in?"

I stepped right back. I knew that it would be very cold if I fell in. Still, I loved to look at the water. It was like looking into my mother's jewelry box-- all sparkles and spangles.

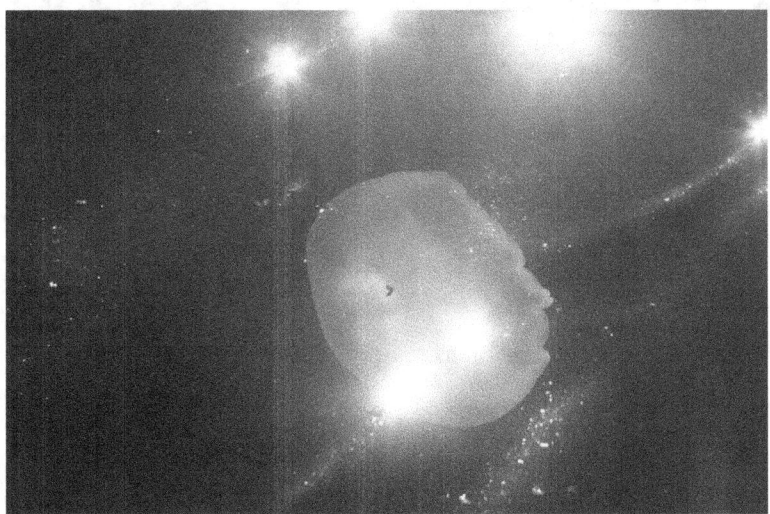

I looked up at my mother to tell her about the water. But her face was all squinched up. She was thinking. I pretended that her face was play-doh, and I could just press all those pinches and squinches right out of it. I crossed the deck and climbed onto the seat beside her. Gently I pushed on her cheek.

She jumped. "Carla Ann! What are you doing? Can't you see that I'm thinking?" Yes, I could see that. I thought she should stop thinking. She had a beautiful face when she wasn't thinking. She had dark brown eyes and long eyelashes. Her skin was the same color as my teddy bear, and her black hair was long and shiny.

The ferry headed out across the inlet. It's called a foot ferry, because they only let you get on with your feet -- no cars allowed. Mom likes to stay inside the cabin on the ferry and read her school books. I like to go outside and look at the water. Every morning we discuss it. Sometimes she gets mad, and we stay inside. Sometimes she just sighs, and we go outside.

I could see Bremerton and the ferry dock. Soon we would have to get off. Then we would take a bus to college, and Mom would go to class, and I would go to the daycare. I like my daycare at the college. I have another daycare I go to when Mom is working. I don't like that as much. It 's in a lady's house and she yells too much. Next year I'll go to school, like Mom. That scares me. "Mom?" I patted her on the arm, so she would stop thinking. "Mom? When I go to school will my face get all squinched, too?"

She blinked and turned to look at me. "Will your face what?"

"Will my face get pinched like scrumpled up play-doh?"

"Why are you asking me that?"

Then she was looking at me too much, like she might be going to get mad.

"Nothing. Never mind." I looked out at the water. The big ferry, the ferry that takes cars to Seattle, was passing us.

"Carla, tell me now why you asked me that."

I wiggled and waggled in my seat. "I just wondered if I would have to think when I go to school."

I could see she had all her thoughts on me now, like I was one of her school books. "I certainly hope you'll think when you go to school. Are you asking me this because I think when I go to school? And my face gets wrinkled up when I think? Is that it?" The wind blew her hair back. "Is that why you were touching my face just now?"

"I just wanted to smooth the pinches out." I watched a seagull fly by. "I like your face without the pinches. "

She sighed. She rubbed and scrubbed at her face. Then she looked at me and smiled. "There; is that better?"

I smiled back at her. "Yeah!"

"I like my face better without squinches, too, honeybun. I just can't study without squinching, I guess."

"Do you have to study on the ferry?"

She looked at me for a long time, and I saw her thoughts go away. I thought she had forgotten about me. Then she said, "No." She smiled at me. "No, fifteen minutes isn't going to make that much difference. I won't study on the ferry anymore." Her face was beautiful.

Our ferry bumped and thumped up against the dock. We went inside and lined up to get off. The ferry man, Jim, took my hand and helped me jump onto the dock. I didn't need his help, but he liked to do it. I went to the rail and looked over.

"Carla! Come on! We'll miss our bus!" She always said that, but we never did. I hurried after her, trying to look for jellyfish at the same time. Then I saw one! It looked like a runny fried egg, sunny side up, with that goopy white stuff hanging down around the side.

"Look, Mom, look! A jellyfish!"

"Oh, Carla, please --" My mother came over to me and grabbed my hand.

"But, Mom, look!" I pointed at the jellyfish. She stopped and looked at me. She looked at the jellyfish.

"The bus isn't here yet, is it?" she asked.

"No, Mom."

"We can look at the jellyfish for a minute." We both stood at the rail and looked at the jellyfish flowing and floating through the water.

## FAMILY DISCUSSION QUESTIONS

- *How do you decide what is important and what is not?*
- *Do you get impatient when people do not listen to you? What do you do to get someone's attention?*
- *Why did Carla compare her mother's face to play-doh? Do you feel your face change when you are thinking hard?*
- *Do you like to watch jellyfish?*

http://kids.nationalgeographic.com/animals/jellyfish/#jellyfish-tentacles.jpg

# CARSON THE HERON

"I hate waiting," said James.

"Waiting for what?" asked his grandmother, Beverly.

"Anything." James put his backpack down in its place by the door and took his second-best Gandalf robe off the hook. "But especially waiting for Mom to pick me up after school."

"Let's go for a walk, James," said Beverly.

James groaned. "Whenever I complain about something, you take me for a walk." He pulled on his robe with a jerk.

"Exercise helps when you're sad or angry. Believe me, I know."

Beverly sat down, and James helped her put on her shoes. She had a hard time bending over sometimes.

"What do you get angry about, Gran?"

"Getting old. I hate getting old, James."

He looked up into her sky-blue eyes. "But if you weren't old, Gran, you couldn't be my Gran!"

"That's a good point, James, a very good point. I do love being your grandmother. But I don't like being unsteady on my feet, and I don't like being so creaky. And I really, really miss your grandfather."

Beverly stood up and they went out the door together. Beverly walked slowly down the steps to the driveway and slowly along the driveway to the road.

"We'll go to the estuary today, James, I want to show you somebody."

"Such a long walk, " grumbled James.

"Gandalf walked through the mines of Moria."

James nodded. He was using Beverly's walking stick as his Gandalf staff. Beverly didn't need it for the long, flat stretch which led to the estuary.

The estuary was a fingertip of water which seemed to be gently touching the land. The tide was coming in with long, slow ripples which barely stirred the seaweed drifting on the surface.

"There he is," said Beverly softly. She pointed.

"Who?"

"Well, I call him Carson, because he reminds me of the butler in Downton Abbey. Very nice but -- you know -- very stately."

James looked out, and sure enough, there was a dignified-looking bird standing very upright and still in the shallow water. "What is he?"

"A great blue heron."

"What's he doing?"

"Fishing."

James chuckled. "He doesn't have a pole."

"No, he has his beak. And a very great deal of patience. He will wait and wait and wait for a fish to swim near and then -- stab!" Beverly bent forward so quickly she almost lost her balance. She grabbed for her stick. James quickly handed it to her and put a hand under her elbow to steady her. "Thank you," said Beverly, a little breathlessly.

"I'd like to see him catch a fish," said James.

"You will, if you wait patiently."

James sighed. "I hate waiting."

"I know."

They stood silently, watching. The waves curled in. Two sparrows played tag over their heads. Six geese swam past, honking gossip to each other. Beverly leaned on her stick with a little sigh. James asked, "Isn't he ever --"

And then the heron took two steps forward with his long, long legs, and his long neck bent down and his long, thin beak stabbed the water, and he came up with a fish.

He shook the fish and water droplets flew, sparkling in the evening sun. The heron tossed his head back and swallowed half the fish, then shook his head hard again, and swallowed the rest. They could see it slide down his neck. "Why doesn't he choke?" exclaimed James.

"I don't know, but he never does."

The heron resumed his upright stance, as alert as a butler waiting table.

"Now he'll wait again?" asked James.

"Yes."

"He does it every day?"

"He does it twice every day, in the morning and in the evening."

"That's a lot of waiting."

"Yes, but he's watching all the time. He doesn't get bored, because he's interested in everything he sees."

James looked thoughtfully at Carson. "When I'm waiting for Mom, I could be making up new stories for you. About Gandalf."

"That's a very good idea. I love your stories."

"I know."

## FAMILY DISCUSSION QUESTIONS

o   *What do you get angry about? What do you do when you're angry?*
o   *Are you a patient person or an impatient person? What makes you think so?*
o   *Do you like to look at birds?*

http://www.biokids.umich.edu/critters/Ardea_herodias/

# SEAL STORY

Beverley and her grandson James were taking a walk along the drive. They looked out at the boats in the harbor. It was summer, and the air was warm and smelled of fresh-cut grass and hot, salty seaweed. A seal pup lay on the float dock off the neighbor's property.

James was wearing his Gandalf robe, although it was really too warm for the day. He carried his grandmother's walking stick, pretending it was his wizard's staff. He shook it at the seal pup. "Begone, or I shall send fireworks at you!" he cried.

"Don't do that," said Beverly sharply.

James looked at her in surprise. "What's wrong, Gran?"

"You'll scare him into the water, and then his mother won't know where to find him." Beverly stopped, panting a little, and put her hand out for her stick. James handed it to her. He knew she needed to "get her wind."

Beverly leaned on the stick, and they looked out at the seal pup, who returned their stare with his big, shiny brown eyes. "She's left him while she forages for her lunch. She'll come back for him soon."

"How do you know?" The pup was silvery gray, with spots.

"She told me." James started to laugh and then he didn't.

Beverly nodded at him approvingly. "Not with words. With her eyes. I saw her one day last week. She was just about to dive into the water and leave him, and she looked at me. It was the same look I gave people when your mother was young. It is the look which says, 'This is my child. You leave him alone or you will deal with me.'"

"Does my mom have that look?"

"Every mother does."

"I've never seen it," said James, a little angrily.

Beverly shifted position, putting more of her weight on the stick. "Of course not. The look is for other people, not your own children. James, are you angry at your mother about something?"

"I have to go to daycare after school. I hate it."

"Your mother can't be home in the afternoon anymore."

"The kids at the daycare laugh at me when I am Gandalf. Why doesn't my mother give *them* that look?"

"Have you told her about it?"

"No…. She should just know."

"She is not a wizard, James. She is only a human woman. You have to tell her things."

James sighed. "It's easy to tell you, Gran, but it's hard to tell Mom."

"Would you rather be left home alone, like the seal pup?"

"No." James looked out at the pup. "He looks scared. And lonely. I'll bet he'd rather be with other seals."

"Even if they tease him?"

Before James could answer, a shiny, wet head broke the surface next to the dock and the mama seal threw herself up onto the dock next to her son. She looked over at Beverly and James. "She's giving us the look, Gran!"

"Yes, we'd better move along." Beverly turned around. "I think I need to go home, James."

"Does your hip hurt?"

"Yes. It's a battle I fight every day."

"You fight battles?"

"Not like Gandalf," Beverly sighed. "It's not magic. Well, maybe it is. I hurt and I ache, but I come out for a walk anyway. I get tired, but I feel better. Inside."

James thought for awhile. "I will fight to be Gandalf, Gran. Even if it hurts. Because that's who I am -- inside."

"Good. That's very good thinking, James."

"I know."

## FERRY FINDINGS

**FAMILY DISCUSSION QUESTIONS**

o   *Have you ever seen a mother protect her child?*

o   *Do you sometimes have to fight to be you? Is it hard?*

o   *Have you ever seen a seal or a sea lion?*

http://education.nationalgeographic.org/activity/seals-versus-sea-lions/

## HUCKLEBERRY HORIZON

Oh, for some of those pills now, she thought. Energy pills she had called them. Tiny, translucent, and orange-red, they gave a sour squirt when bitten. She had gathered them in small cups -- the dosage, after all, had not needed to be large. She would offer them to the adults, not entirely as a joke, to imbue them with what she had had then -- the enthusiasm for boundless activity.

She remembered how the hard-packed earth would puff dust as she ran down to the water. Look at that calico scene with young eyes blind to the beauty! See only the potentialities! Greens of salal and Oregon grape, browns of earth and evergreen trunks, shimmers of golden sunbeam dancers-- all lost to her eye for the glorious liquid playground to be enjoyed.

Dancing with the sunbeams -- the lake was her love, her playmate, her favorite pet. The quintessential companion, it fit her every mood.

Energy pills! She would take them back to the drooping and panting adults, forcing the pills into their hands, crying, "Come swim! Come play!"

It was strange to her; the pills always worked, although they were never eaten.

Hot August days followed by cool mountain nights enjoyed in cozy sleeping bags. The bodies of family, guest(s), pet(s) all in one large tent, sharing the warmth and companionship.

Mornings she would awaken to see the shadows of the vine maples on the white tent roof, shimmering with the early breeze. The cool mornings were for raking and digging and planting and rock piling -- and anticipating the afternoon.

She sighed. How easy it had seemed then to work the morning (so slowly!) away, and how much vim she had had left for play afterward. There had been no bottom to her well of vitality then, but now... Now, after a morning of vacuuming the apartment, picking up toys, doing laundry, planning meals -- she found it hard to face an afternoon of anything, let alone more of the same. She looked out at the grey skies of October and didn't see that the ash trees were donning new colors. She could only remember --

Those glorious afternoons! Jumping into the water -- Oh, what a shock that freezing run-off was to heat-slick skin. But then the body adjusted to the velvet shimmer as the legs kicked and the arms pumped and the blood raced warmly through. Splashing siblings sent millions of crystals glittering into the air. Slow adults would join them (were they only feigning their reluctance?) gasping on entry, then laughing, exhaustion forgotten in the snapping shift to a new environment.

Riding logs, diving off rafts, sinking air mattresses, all paled before the supreme satisfaction of sneaking up on someone dry and warm and sending forth a blast of chilliness from an eager hand.

The afternoon would shimmer (so quickly!) away. The adults would remember the work done and the work yet to do and would pull themselves laboriously up out of the water. And finally, under orders and last of all, she would remove herself from the easy buoyancy of her friend.

The sun would slip down, the mountains like an enormous fan before its face. Her wet feet would pick up the yellow-brown earth as she trudged the long, steep way back to the tent and dinner.

As the crickets chittered, she would urge the others to finish dinner and dishes. On to the next activity! Light the campfire! Find the marshmallows! A twig was carefully chosen, music books were unearthed, and as the fire flared a cacophony of inexperienced voices would rise in the twilight. Squirrels and raccoons doubtless put their paws over their ears and looked at the moon, hoping for a few coyotes to drown out the noise of those intrusive humans.

She smiled at the whimsical thought as she stepped out on the small patio and checked on the progress of her small son's unsteady steps through the damp grass. She hoped he would stay away from the blackberries. She didn't want to have to go racing after him to pull him away from the brambles. She didn't have the energy.

She berated that self of yesteryear. Why hadn't she been more cognizant then? Always, she had been immured, unthinking, in the moment of zealous activity -- or else she had been anticipating, urging, yanking at time for the next joy to come. Stop, child of yesterday! Seize the moment! Gather the rosebuds!

She sighed.

That long ago child could only await the delight and endure the endless waiting.

She looked at her son and saw how his small shoes barely showed above the grass. He had almost outgrown them, his first pair of shoes. When had he grown so big?

Suddenly she was plunged into that freezing lake again, feeling that same shock of awareness and startled gasp for breath. For what was she doing now, wishing for energy pills and dreaming of the past, but ignoring the now, never to know it again? Look at your own child, woman! Listen to the swish of his jacket as his small arms swing, and his chubby legs pump so vehemently, and he squeals with the joy of independent motion. Meet his dimples with your own and recognize his wordless plea for you to come and play! Stop thinking about what to fix for dinner and when to mop the floor. You don't need energy pills! Remember, they were never eaten. And why not?

Because it was the giver who supplied the energy. And it was the attitude of the receiver which made the transaction possible.

She laughed with the joy of discernment. She remembered the adults surreptitiously dropping the sour red berries to the ground, only to rise with renewed vitality -- garnered from love for the giver.

She threw her head back and saw the gold and yellow and orange and red of the trees and whispered, "Look to your own child for your medication, foolish adult!"

And she did look, and he was running to her with his small hands full of laboriously uprooted blue sailors. So she crouched down to gather in son and sailors, and she sniffed deeply of her rose -- which strongly resembled the smell of crisp October breezes and a damp diaper.

**FAMILY DISCUSSION QUESTIONS**

- *Who is "she"? Why is she unhappy at the beginning?*
- *What does "she" suddenly realize when her son runs up to her at the end?*
- *There is an old poem which says: "Gather ye rosebuds while ye may." What do you think that means?*

https://www.poets.org/poetsorg/poem/virgins-make-much-time

# NEW HEADING

Ramona stood, apprehensively watching her mother approach. The wind whipped her mother's white silk blouse aside, showing the outline of her lace-trimmed bra. Her mother's carefully cut and permed black hair was whipped into Medusa's snarls. Her face could turn Ramona to stone.

"So." Her mother stopped, her balance unsteady as her heels sank into the turf. "You thought you would abandon me, too."

Ramona felt the stoniness creep through her body. The wind pulled her hair, flinging it out of her collar bit by bit, sending it snapping at her cheeks.

"Nothing to say? Isn't that just typical." Her mother's voice snapped like the wind. "At least when your father left, he had the courtesy to tell me first. At least when your brother left, he showed his anger in all sorts of ways first. It was almost a relief to have him go. But you. You would just slide silently out of my life like a snake, wouldn't you?"

Ramona was held, ossified by her mother's pain, unable to speak.

"Isn't this enough for you?" Her mother made a sweeping motion with one white clad arm, the silk billowing against her side. The gold chains around her neck sparkled in the afternoon sun. "This house, a pool, a car of your own, private school of your choice, even your own boat, for God's sake -- What more could you want?" She put a hand to her throat. "What more could *they* have wanted?" Her mother stopped, words swallowed by Ramona's silence. "I don't know why I talk to you. I just want to take you by the throat and shake you. " Her fists clenched and unclenched. She swiped at her face with one hand, then turned and stumbled across the lawn to the house.

Tears came, hot on her cold cheeks, and melted Ramona's face. She sat down and whispered to the new spring grass all that she had wanted to say. After a while, she got out her cell phone. Shivering, she asked Dan, "Who told her?"

"Not me."

"I know it wasn't you, Dan. You won't even look at my mother, let alone talk to her. Was it Jenny or Chris?"

"I don't know."

"Dan, you never lie to me."

"I'm not lying now. I don't know... for sure."

"But you know who it probably was. Was it probably Chris?"

"He did mention it. He was very worried about you, Ramona. We all were. Are."

"Preserve me from your worry." She disconnected and stood up. She was too cold to do anything but go back to the house. She went in the back and up to her room, took a shower in her bathroom and put on her Mickey Mouse bathrobe which was getting threadbare from washings. Her father had gotten her the robe when she was twelve. That was before the investment windfall which had made them wealthy. The trip to Disneyland and the thick terrycloth robe had been an extravagance then. Ramona often wondered what their lives would have been like if her mother had not invested in that software company.

A cartoon villain -- that was what her mother had become. A crazy, scheming sea witch who thought she knew what was best for everyone because she had made a ton of money -- not just for their family, but for all her clients. Soon she had more clients than she could handle, and she hired staff and decided she needed to "upscale." She bought the waterfront house and the yacht and brought home brochures for private schools. Ramona and her brother were happy enough to switch schools in exchange for new wardrobes, new phones, new everything -- and when they were old enough, their own cars. Why not?

Their father had moved more and more into the background, his salary as an electrician a meaningless trickle in their lives. There weren't any big fights. Their father had just faded from the scene. He had no role in the new prosperity. Every job he had performed, from handyman to tutor to counselor, was being done by hired hands. He had just quietly said goodbye one day and moved away, claiming nothing from his former life but the right to see his children when he could. But then he got a job five hundred miles away in Montana, and they never saw him.

That had been five years ago. In the two years following, Ramona's brother had been kicked out of one private school, and then another and another. He had had raging quarrels with their mother and crashed his car twice. He had been in juvenile detention and bailed out. Their mother had screamed at him that she would never do it again. Seventeen by then, he had left.

Now Ramona was seventeen, and she was going to leave, too.

Her phone buzzed.

"Ramona, you know I didn't tell your mom, right? Because I didn't. I wouldn't do that to you, you know that, right? Even though I am worried about you and mad at you for thinking of going away."

Ramona could picture Jenny's cell on speaker, Jenny's hands flying around, like agitated starlings. "I know that, Jenny."

"Oh! Well, that's good. But I'll just hate going through senior year without you, Ramona. Who'll help me with my French?"

"I have to go, Jenny. Talk to you later. " Ramona checked her email, but there was no response yet to her query. She had seen the ad on

Craig's List: Wanted: Nanny for one 12-year-old boy. Must be willing to travel. Must speak French.

She had smiled and murmured: *"L'evasion du prisonnie...* the escape of a prisoner…"

When she had told her friends about it, they had been horrified. "You applied for a job?" Jenny had demanded. "Why?"

"Does this mean you'll pay income tax?" Dan had asked. His short black hair seemed to bristle. "How could you?"

"Are you really that good at French?" asked Chris. "What did your mother say?"

Ramona sipped some soda, then said, "I want to do something, go places, be somebody."

"Oh, no," groaned Chris. "You can't mean you want to find yourself! My Dad is trying to get me to do that all the time!"

"I just want to get out of here. I need to." Ramona looked past them, out the window at the bay. The sun was sparkling on the water of Puget Sound, reminding her of the diamonds in her mother's rings.

"Well, you don't need to work!" cried Jenny. "Tell your mom you want to go to France on an exchange program. You know she'll spring for it." Crumbs flew from the donut in her hand as she gestured, teasing the seagulls loitering outside.

"Did you talk to your mom?" asked Chris.

"No, and I don't intend to." Ramona clenched her jaw. Drifting was something she did with grace and ease. Asserting herself -- that came hard.

"Well, I don't understand this at all," said Jenny, tossing her head. The golden hair on half her head tossed with her; the orange hair on the other half was too short. Jenny preferred to be a few steps behind the current fashion, just to prove she didn't care.

"I applaud your rebellion, but I question your method," said Dan, frowning and tapping his fingers on his bagel. "Wouldn't it bug your mom a lot more for you to throw a few wild parties at the house when she's gone? When I want my mum to sit up and take notice, I just invite a few guys over in saggy pants. It scares her. I'd be glad to give you some names."

"I am not trying to get revenge on my mother. At least I don't think I am." Ramona chewed on her straw, wondering about this.

"What about us?" asked Jenny. "We need you."

Her anxiety drew Ramona's eyes away from the window. "We'll be splitting up soon anyway, Jen. Next year we'll all be in different cities."

"No!" said Jenny. "I want you to go to college with me!"

"And what about college?" asked Chris. "You can't just walk away from your future."

"My future is exactly what I want to escape," said Ramona.

"Very existential," said Dan admiringly.

"Very ridiculous," said Chris. "College is just a way of postponing the future. Your parents support you while you stack up the credits. You can walk away from it all later."

"College is the cauldron where the most radical new ideas are brewed," said Dan. "I plan to start the next world-shaking 'ism' while I'm at UCLA."

Ramona smiled at them. "I love you all, but I can't be like you. I need to know where I'm headed." She gathered up her purse and jacket. "I want to travel, see a different world than the one I'm living in. Learn for myself. By myself."

"Looking after a twelve-year-old boy?" asked Jenny, pressing her brilliantly pink lips together. "I think you're just trying to replace your brother. Your family."

"Well, what if I am?"


When she had gotten home, her mother had been waiting on the newly fertilized lawn.


Her email pinged. The family of the twelve-year-old wanted to interview her in Seattle. She agreed. Her phone buzzed: Chris. "Ramona, I'm sorry I told your mom, but I just had to ---"

She disconnected.

Disconnected. That was how she felt inside. Disconnected from everyone and everything. She was so tired -- no, exhausted -- from trying so hard to connect with her mother, her friends, her privileged world. None of it -- none of them -- seemed to have any connection to what she was -- deep down inside -- Ramona.

She pulled on a sweatshirt and a windbreaker and walked down to their private dock, listening to the boat squeaking against its floats and to the waves sucking up under the pilings. Maybe Jenny was right. Maybe she was just trying to replace her brother. Maybe she was trying to find her whole family again -- or a better one. Slapping angrily at her tears, she stared into the water. A couple of jellyfish floated there. Seagulls swooped past, arguing over a clam one carried in its beak.

Climbing aboard her boat, she immediately donned her life jacket. It had taken many and varied classes to prove to her mother she was capable of taking care of herself on the water -- water safety, first aid, beginning , intermediate and advanced sailing, and of course, years and years of swimming lessons.

She raised the sail, allowing it to luff, dropped the rudder, and cast off, then leaned back with the tiller under her arm. The wind popped into the sail and her hair slapped into her face. Twisting her hair up, she shoved it into the hood of her sweatshirt, then pushed the tiller over and leaned away from the tilt of the boat as it picked up speed.

The bow lifted and her worries seemed to fly away behind her as the water slapped up over the side and soaked her arm. She concentrated on the sailing, feeling the water thrum against the bottom of the boat, lifting her face to the wind. She blanked her mind to all but the activity, pushing her skill to it limits.

She sailed until her face was sticky with salt water, and her new sneakers were soaked. The wind had picked up, and her arms were getting tired. She sailed around the point, heading for home, running with the sail flung wide. Within seconds of reaching the dock, she cut hard to starboard, put the bow into the wind and the boat stopped, the waves slapping up against it. Ramona felt the tired exuberance she always felt after a good sail. The physical workout, the sea air, the knowledge that she had done something difficult with skill -- it was the only time she felt whole.

When she got to her room, she showered in her bathroom, then logged on to her computer while she dried her hair. The father of the twelve-year-old had just confirmed their appointment at a restaurant in Seattle the following day, Saturday. She went to bed, wondering if she would really go through with it.

A short, plump man took Ramona's hand when they met at the restaurant. "Hello, Ramona, I'm Gene Raskell. I apologize for the rush, but we have plane tickets for Greece next week. We thought we had a nanny lined up, but she developed whooping cough of all things, and won't be going anywhere for a while. " He was still holding her hand. She pulled it gently away. Come meet my wife."

Mrs. Raskell wore a blue silk skirt and a gold and white cashmere sweater. The jingling and sparkling of her jewelry reminded Ramona of her mother. "Hello, Ramona," she said with a faintly Southern drawl. "You are a little younger looking than I had anticipated."

"I'm twenty-one," said Ramona, and pulled out her fake ID for the server. She ordered a glass of the white wine she had heard her mother order recently. Ramona had dressed deliberately in a tailored chambray dress. She wanted to look professional and older than she was, but she didn't want to look too wealthy to need this job.

"I'm sure my husband told you we are a little rushed. He has a business meeting in Greece, and then we are going on to France. Would you be able to leave next week?"

"Yes," said Ramona. "I'm between jobs right now."

"Your written references were excellent, although we have been unable to speak to them personally."

"They are busy people."

Mr. Raskell was nothing like her father. He talked a lot and kept touching her arm. When Ramona asked to meet their son, they both seemed surprised and a little uneasy.

"He's just a typical twelve-year-old," said Mrs. Raskell.

"There won't be time," said Mr. Raskell. "He's at a boarding school in Massachusetts. We'll pick him up on our way."

Ramona found the contract in her inbox when she got home. She had a job. The open window let in the early spring breeze, and the sound of the waves. The boy must have been expelled from his boarding school. Ramona recognized that look in Mrs. Raskell's eyes: What are we going to do with him now? She had seen the look in her mother's eyes many times. And why else would they be taking a twelve-year-old to Europe before the school year was over? Mr. Raskell would be a problem, too. Did she really want to do this?

She stood and looked out the window, breathing deeply of salty air and fish and seaweed. The tide was high, and the moon shone on the water, a long trail of light, beckoning to her. Her boat would be pulling at its tether, like an impatient puppy wanting a walk. She pulled on jeans and a sweatshirt, wool socks and old canvas shoes. She zipped up her windbreaker and stepped out onto her deck. She paused at the top of the stairs and looked back.

Her guardian angel night light glowed dimly by her bed. She went back into her room and got her overnight bag out of the closet. She packed it with jeans and sweatshirts, underwear and socks and shoes, the chambray dress and a skirt and a blouse and a sweater. She took her wallet out of her purse and put it into the pocket of her windbreaker. She had withdrawn as much as she was allowed today. She would use her credit cards until her mother cut her off. She got her oldest photo album off the bookshelf and put it into the side pocket of the bag. She tried to fit a large stuffed cat into the other pocket, but it wouldn't fit. She hugged the cat, and put it down on the bed. She slung the bag over her shoulder, switched off her guardian angel, and went out into the night.

She had never sailed in the middle of the night before. It wasn't safe, and her mother would never have allowed it.

At first it was exciting, knowing she was absolutely alone. The stars were tremendous and the waves patted the boat as if they were congratulating her. But after a while, the chill cut deep, and the black emptiness disturbed her. It reminded her of the way she had felt when her father had left, and again when her brother had slammed out of the house. Alone.

She tacked in closer to the shore, then realized she wasn't sure where she was. She had never realized that the lights at night would all look so much the same. The panic rose up in her throat, but her time in safety classes paid off. She remembered how to navigate by the stars.

She found the Little Dipper and set course for the marina. There were other lights on the water now. The Seattle ferry was unmistakable, and a few fishing boats. She could hear voices and the squeak of nets being winched. She saw the lights lining the marina dock. Dan lived near here. Ramona smiled. She pushed the tiller over, the boom swung past her face, and she headed for the marina.

She docked at the slip her mother paid for and walked to Dan's house. It was easy to wake him without disturbing his family, because his bedroom was over the detached garage. She was so glad to enter his warm room. Dan was less glad to see her.

"What did you think you were doing? Where were you going to go?" Dan rubbed his bristly head and then his bristly cheeks. He looked like a confused and sleepy porcupine. He wore a t-shirt and boxers and seemed embarrassed. He pulled on a pair of sweatpants.

"I just had to get out of there, Dan. I had to." She pulled off her damp windbreaker.

"Yes, but --- what now?"

"That's what I'm trying to decide." She sat down at his desk. "That's why I came to you. You're sensible."

"Sensible!" He was outraged. "I'm an anarchist!"

"Exactly. You understand that I want to reject the life my mother has made for me. But those people, Dan -- the Raskells -- they aren't any different. They aren't a family, either!" She turned away from him, her throat tight. Dan could stand being insulted, but he hated tears. "You know, I passed fishermen on the way here, and I was jealous of them. Fishermen! because they are useful, and wanted."

"Not by the fish." Dan shook his head. "I need some coffee. Want some?"

"No, thanks. Dan, don't you want to be useful and wanted?"

"What? Are you saying I'm not?" Dan turned his coffee maker on and found a mug under a shirt on the floor. "Ramona, I am the most useful and wanted person I know! I think you are confusing making money with being useful and that's natural, considering your mother." He looked under the bed and pulled out a bag of chips. "Want some?"

She shook her head. "You mean I can be useful without making money… doing charity work or whatever…"

"NO!" Dan sat on the bed and waved a chip in the air. "NO! Not charity. Charity is the last refuge of the guilty rich. I am useful because I remind people that these things we take for granted are ONLY things we take for granted. Subvert the dominant paradigm!"

Ramona smiled. "Didn't Mr. Schuhart say that was a fallacy?"

"Mr. Schuhart works for the school district. They make their living from the dominant paradigm. I can teach freely, because I am part of no system. I am wanted by all, yet I make not a cent for anyone."

Ramona laughed. "That's fine for you, but I don't think I can teach anyone anything."

"Everyone can teach something. Let's think about this for a moment. What do you know?" Dan cleaned out his coffee mug with his shirt.

"Uh, well, I know how to sail."

"What about something a little more esoteric. What do you know about money?"

He poured coffee into the mug.

"It doesn't make you happy," said Ramona so quickly she surprised herself.

"Ahh! Not many people know that. What do you know about… family?"

"I need one." Again, the swift answer surprised her.

"Okay, what do you know about family survival?"

Ramona had to think about that. "You need to talk. Families need to talk. " She shook her head and her hair fell down from the inside of her hood. She realized she had finally warmed up. She pulled off the sweatshirt. "But it's too late for my family. And it's too late for me. I don't think anybody wants me. I need to be somebody new."

"Ha!" barked Dan. "You sound like that kid's book -- you know, the *Put Me in the Zoo* guy. You remember what happened to him? No? Your education is sadly lacking. He discovered that his friends wanted him to just the way he was. Just like I want you the way you are. And Jenny does."

Dan rolled up the empty chip bag and pitched it at the garbage can. He missed. He looked at Ramona sideways. "I'm a lousy basketball player, but a good judge of people. And I bet your Mom wants you. I think she'd even talk to you. What would you talk about?" He sipped his coffee. "Not that I'm recommending communication between parents and offspring, mind you. I think it's very dangerous, myself. But I'm just following your answers logically here. You want a family and families should talk, so what do you want to say?"

Ramona made Dan get dressed and drive her home. She wanted to be there before her mother found out she was gone. She let herself into the house, careful not to bump her bag on the vase of flowers just inside the door. But when she tiptoed up the hall to her room, she could see a faint glow. Her guardian angel had been switched on.

Her mother was sitting on the bed, looking out at the water. Ramona approached her warily, putting her bag down and shrugging out of her windbreaker. Her mother stood up slowly and as she turned, Ramona could see the sparkle of tears on her cheeks and the stuffed cat in her arms. Ramona went to her and hugged her, with the cat squashed between them.

For now, anyway, there really wasn't anything she wanted to say.

## FAMILY DISCUSSION QUESTIONS

- *Have you ever been really angry at a member of your family? What did you do?*
- *How important are your things to you? Is there any thing which you simply could not live without? (Not counting food and a place to live!)*
- *Do you know where you are headed?*
- *Ramona goes out in her boat alone at night. Have you ever done something dangerous that you knew you shouldn't? Why did you do it?*

http://www.boatingsidekicks.com/

# IT'S MAGIC

The man standing on the beach looked out at the waves; the wind whipped his pants tight against his thin legs, and he shivered, but he didn't leave. He had lived near Puget Sound all of his eighty years, but he had never really *looked* at its temperamental waters when he had been young.

There was something magical about water that could look so dangerous on a fall day like this and so friendly in the summer. The man smiled. Magic. He had thought magic unimportant, once. He might never have seen the water if it had not been for a magic trick many years before...

He stood at the kitchen counter eating his toast, reviewing his agenda for the day.

Sometimes his son would get up, too, and they would smile at each other as his son fixed himself some cereal.

"Can you help me with my spelling words, Dad?"

"Sorry I can't, son. I have to catch the ferry. I'm sure your mother will help you."

"Okay, Dad. Have a good day." His son would switch on the TV.

The man liked his early mornings on the ferry. He liked the peace of the fog on the water. He liked sitting by the window, sipping his coffee, scanning the newspaper.

He liked his work. Being a stockbroker was challenging, and he was good at it. He brought in a very respectable income, but more importantly (he told himself), he was making a contribution to society. He always intended to end his day by five, but somehow there was always one more task to accomplish, a loose end or two to take care of. He seldom caught his homebound ferry before seven. He would arrive home in time to say good night to his son.

"Tomorrow night could you read me a story, Dad?"

"Sure, son, tomorrow night I'll get home earlier and we'll read a story or play a game -- whatever you want."

His son would smile his gap-toothed smile as the man turned out the light. After their child was settled, the man and his wife would sit in the living room, watching TV, reading, and talking. The man would listen to his wife talk about her part-time job and the things she had done around the house. He tried to let her know that he valued her contribution to their lives. What she did was necessary, and he wanted her to be happy. The orderliness of his life was disturbed when she was not happy.

One evening, however, his wife reported something different. "They've offered me a full-time position at the gift shop."

"Mmm, yes? That's very nice, dear. It shows they value you as an employee."

"I've decided to accept." She was working on some sort of tole-painted figures, to be sold in the gift shop, the man assumed.

He put his newspaper down. "Accept? But what about me? What about the boy?"

She laughed. "You don't spend more than two waking hours with us anymore. During the week, anyway." She dangled a farmer's wife by her wire hook.

He was shocked. "But I'm providing for us! And very well!"

She put down the wife and picked up a wooden cow. "Yes, I know you are. And that's why I haven't wanted to complain. Because I love living here on the island, and I am so happy not to have to worry about money as we did when we were young. But I'm bored and lonely during the week! And I've figured everything out. You don't have to do a thing. I've arranged for our son to go next door for the hour that he'll be home and I won't" She finished the cow and picked up a pig.

"But-- what about the house? You're always saying how difficult it is to keep clean."

"I've found a cleaning service to come in. I don't know why I didn't think of it earlier." She finished the pig and picked up a farmer.

"I don't like it," said the man, trying to think of another rational objection.

"I know you don't, honey, and I'm sorry. I know change is hard for you, but I promise-- you won't notice a thing." She jammed a wire hook into the head of the farmer, then put him back into the box.

The cleaner was hired, the boy began spending his afternoons at the neighbor's, and the wife seemed very happy. The boy seemed happy, too; he was best friends with the neighbor's son.

Only the man was unhappy, and he didn't know why. The thing that he had feared most, that his daily routine would change, hadn't happened. When he got up in the morning he ate his toast, and when his son got up, they smiled at each other. His son would fix his bowl of cereal and then start working on something. He didn't turn on the TV. He didn't ask his father to do anything.

The man might venture a comment: "Sorry I can't stay, son, but I have to catch the ferry. "

His son wouldn't look up. "Bye, Dad."

When he got home at night and said good night, his son didn't ask him anything. "I'll try to get home earlier tomorrow night."

"That's okay, Dad."

When he went out to the living room, his wife wasn't reading or watching TV. "I got behind on my paperwork today," she would say with a smile. "I'll be staying up a little late. Go to bed when you feel like it, honey. I know that you have to get up early." She would kiss him and sit at the kitchen table, papers spread out before her. The overhead light would shine on her hair.

One morning the boy got up and didn't even fix breakfast, but immediately began working on something. "What are you working on, Son?"

His son's tongue was between his teeth, and he was whispering to himself. "What? It's just something I need to practice."

"Would you like some help?"

His son looked up, plainly shocked. "Do *you* know magic, Dad?"

"Magic! Of course not. Magic is just a – just a trick!"

"That's right, Dad. I don't think you can help. Thanks, anyway."

The man frowned. "Did you get your homework done?"

"Yes."

"Well. Don't forget to have breakfast."

"I won't. Bye, Dad."

The man always took the afternoon of his son's parent-teacher conference off. School was a priority with him, he would tell his colleagues. But usually he would go with his wife, and she would talk to the teacher about their son's homework habits and health. This time his wife had asked him to go alone. She had an appointment at work. Reminding himself to find time to talk to his wife about her priorities, the man sat down next to the teacher's desk and looked at his son's schoolwork.

"Your son's reading and math skills have changed this quarter. Have you been doing something different lately?"

"Ahh, well. My wife is working full-time and unfortunately our son has to go to a neighbor's after school. I think it may not be a good idea."

"Oh, that's right! He told me about that. I don't think I made myself clear. Your son's scores have improved!"

"Oh, well... that's fine! I wasn't sure about that neighbor arrangement."

"I don't think there could be a better caretaker for your son than your neighbor. He is wonderful with children. He volunteers here every Friday."

"He? He works here?"

"He volunteers, yes. He has a home-based business, so he can make time for the things he thinks are important. He says that school is a priority for him. The children love him. He does magic tricks for them." The teacher smiled. " Your son is doing very well." She handed him a stack of papers and said good bye. The man walked out in a daze. He drove home in a daze. He sat in the kitchen in a daze.

His son -- his son!-- was improving his school scores by working with another boy's father. His son was learning magic tricks from another boy's father. His son was learning at school with another boy's father. By the time his wife got home, the man had decided what needed to be done.

"You'll have to quit your job," he told his wife.

"Pardon me?" she asked as she put down her briefcase. "Did you go to the conference? Is he doing poorly?"

"He's doing very well, but you didn't tell me that this neighbor who's caring for him is a man."

"What difference does that make?" She raised one eyebrow. He hated that. The man paced the kitchen. "Ahh, well, what if he's some sort of pervert?"

"Whatever gave you that idea? Is that what the teacher said?"

"No."

"Doesn't he volunteer at the school?"

"Yes."

"Well, then he's been fingerprinted and checked out by the state patrol. What is your problem?"

He watched her walk to the sink and pour herself a glass of water. She was wearing a red jacket and a red skirt, and she looked very beautiful and very competent. She acted and sounded very competent. He didn't like it. "I don't like it." She laughed. "Well, you'll have to have a better reason than that to get me to quit my job." She put her glass in the sink and went into the bedroom to change.

He was still staring blankly into space when their son walked in. "Hi, Dad! It's weird seeing you home this early!"

The man stared at him helplessly, wanting to scream and shout, "I don't like it!" But his son's open happiness made him dumb. His son was almost up to his shoulder! His son was becoming a person, with his own thoughts and ideas. The man realized that he didn't know his son at all.

"You okay, Dad?"

" Ahh, yes. Yes, son, I think I'm fine. I think I'll be much better, but... I'm fine. And I'd love to see one of your magic tricks."

A loud, deep-toned horn startled the old man. He stumbled on the rocky beach and nearly lost his balance. "Damn ferry horn," he muttered. He glanced around to see if anyone had been watching him. Old age could be so embarrassing. Caroline was always telling him not to walk on the rocks anymore.

As he tried to negotiate his way up the beach to the parking lot, he thought perhaps she was right. He finally made it back to the car, where Caroline surveyed him critically.

"You got your pants wet."

He put his arm around her. "I'm glad you took that full-time job."

" What? Are you senile? I haven't worked full-time in over fifteen years."

"I know."

She looked at him suspiciously, then leaned into his arm. "You certainly weren't glad at the time!"

"No, I wasn't. The water made me think of it."

"You are senile." But she said it softly, and she turned her head to give him a kiss. The walk-on passengers began to debark. He searched eagerly for his son. To his annoyance, Caroline spotted him first.

"Andrew! Here we are! Andrew!" She waved wildly.

"For heaven's sake, Caroline, he's not in the next county! You don't need to screech!"

She ignored him as the young man reached them and put his overnight bag down. She drew Andrew into her arms. Andrew looked at his father over his mother's shoulder. "Hi, Dad," he said with a grin -- no longer gap toothed, but still, the man thought, basically the same. When his mother released him, Andrew stuck his hand out to his father. The man took his son's hand and pulled him into his arms. He knew what was important.

## FAMILY DISCUSSION QUESTIONS

- *This story has a "flashback." The father is remembering a long time ago. Have you ever gotten lost in a flashback?*
- *The father has a hard time telling his wife and son how he feels. Have you ever had trouble talking about your feelings? Why was it hard?*
- *Have you ever done a magic trick? Do you think you would like to?*

http://www.kidzone.ws/magic/

## ABOUT THE PHOTOGRAPHER

Glenn Wachtman has been a photographer for most of his life, both professional and amateur. He took every photo class he could in high school and college and started working at the local weekly newspaper right out of college. He spent the next several years working his way up the ladder to shoot for a large city daily, and worked as a stringer for Associated Press.

Wachtman has won several awards at several levels, both art and news. As he gets older, he says he's grown to appreciate the artistic aspects of photography more and more.

http://fineartamerica.com/profiles/glenn-wachtman.html

## ABOUT THE AUTHOR

Susan McDonough-Wachtman enjoys throwing her intrepid heroines into unlikely situations. She has published *Snail's Pace* (about a Victorian woman on a spaceship), *Arabella's Gift* (about a medieval woman kidnapped by a dragon), and *Matriarchs* (about a woman from a future matriarchy in a forced marriage to a chauvinistic playboy). Her most recently published book is *Lizzie in the Land Beyond*, about a typical teen who tries to be the savior of an alien world.

McDonough-Wachtman has been writing since grade school, trying her hand at children's stories, short stories, romances, historical novels, essays, fantasies, mysteries, science fiction, numerous letters to the editor and a blog called Renaissance Woman.

http://suewrite.wix.com/susanmcdonough

www.ingramcontent.com/pod-product-compliance
Lightning Source LLC
Chambersburg PA
CBHW071539080526
44588CB00011B/1725